Make IT Now —
Bake IT LaTer! #2

~~~~~~~~~~~~~~~~~~~~~~~~~~~~~~~~~~~~

Make Each Dish in The Morning
Then GenTly SeT IT Aside.
Bring IT ForTh ThaT Evening
And Serve Your Guests with Pride!

Table of Contents

Notes

London Chicken

So simple - and so delicious!

24 pieces of chicken (breasts, legs,
  and second joints)
  butter (enough to brown chicken)
¾ lb sliced mushrooms (can use
  canned, drained)
2 cans cream of chicken soup
1 can mushroom soup
  sherry or white wine to taste.
  (about ¼ cup)

Brown the chicken in butter. Then
  brown mushrooms if using fresh
  ones.
Place chicken in a large casserole.
Mix the soups (undiluted) and pour
  over chicken.
Place mushrooms on top.
Refrigerate.
When ready to bake, add wine, cover
  the casserole, and bake at 350° for
  1½ hours.

Serves 12

2

Notes

Savory Sausage Casserole

Inexpensive and Tasty!

1 lb. bulk pork sausage (a good brand <u>not too salty</u>!)
1 cup uncooked rice
2 pkgs. (2 oz. each) dehydrated chicken
  noodle soup
1/4 cup finely chopped onion
1 cup sliced celery
2 1/2 cups water
1 Tblsp. soy sauce
1/2 cup toasted halved or slivered blanched
  almonds

Break apart the sausage and brown it in
an ungreased skillet, pouring off any
excess fat as it accumulates. Remove
from the burner.

Mix together the sausage, rice, soup,
onion, and celery and place in a
2 qt. casserole.

Refrigerate.

When ready to bake, mix soy sauce with
water and add this, with the almonds,
to the casserole. Mix all gently.

Cover and bake at 350 for 1 hour.

Serves 6

3

Notes

Teen Mix

A special favorite of Teenagers - who consume
this in quantity!

4 slices bacon
1/2 large yellow onion, chopped
1 lb. very lean ground beef
1 large can baked beans (1 lb. 12 oz.) undrained
1 large can solid pack Tomatoes, undrained
1 Teasp. Worcestershire Sauce
1/8 Teasp. garlic salt
1 heaping Teasp. granulated sugar
salt & pepper To taste

Cut bacon in strips and cook Them with the
onion in a large heavy kettle like a Dutch oven.
Do not brown bacon until crisp - it should be
barely cooked.

Add ground beef and brown slightly. Drain off all
excess fat.

Add remaining ingredients and stir gently.

Cover kettle and simmer 1 1/4 hours. Stir
occasionally To prevent sticking.

This may be made ahead and reheated for
4 To 6 hungry Teenagers.

Note: If you prefer it less juicy, do not use
all The liquid with canned Tomatoes.

4

Notes

Wild Rice Party Casserole

A special favorite!

2 cups boiling water
2/3 cup uncooked wild rice
1 can chicken rice soup
1 small can mushrooms, undrained
1/2 cup water
1 Teasp. salt
1 bay leaf
1/4 Teasp. each of celery salt, garlic salt,
    pepper, onion salt, and paprika.
3 Tblsp. chopped onion
3 Tblsp. salad oil
3/4 lb lean ground beef

Pour boiling water over rice. Let stand,
    covered, 15 minutes. Drain.
Place rice in a 2 QT. casserole.
Add soup, mushrooms with liquid, water,
    and seasonings. Mix gently and let
    stand a few minutes.
Sauté onions in oil until glossy. Remove
    and add to casserole.
Add meat to frying pan and fry, stirring
    gently until brown and crumbly.
Add to rice and refrigerate.
When ready, bake 2 hours at 325°, covered.

Serves 4

5

Notes

Egg-Asparagus-Mushroom Casserole

A wonderful Friday luncheon dish!.

2 Tblsp. butter
3 Tblsp. flour
1/2 Teasp. prepared brown mustard
1 can mushroom soup
1 large can green asparagus Tips
4 hard cooked eggs, sliced

1/2 cup rice flakes, crushed before measuring
1/4 cup grated American cheese

Melt butter, add flour, and blend well.

Combine mustard with soup and add To
    flour-mixTure. Cook slowly, stirring
    constantly, until Thick.
In a buttered casserole arrange a layer
    of asparagus, Then a layer of eggs
    and some of The sauce. Repeat
    layers until all is used.
Refrigerate - or just set aside.
When ready To bake, combine rice flakes
    and grated cheese and sprinkle over
    The Top.
Place in a 350° oven, uncovered, and
    bake until hot Through - about
    35 minutes.

Serves 5

6

Notes

Norfolk Noodles

Mighty Tasty!

12 oz. wide noodles
  1 cup fresh parsley, chopped
  1 pt. carton cottage cheese - large curd
  1 pt. carton commercial sour cream
  1 Tblsp. Worcestershire sauce
    dash Tobasco
  1 bunch green onions, chopped. Be sure
    To use some of The onion Tops.
½ cup grated sharp cheese
½ Teasp. paprika

Boil noodles according To directions on
  The package. Drain.
While noodles are still hot, mix in all
  The remaining ingredients except
  cheese and paprika.
Place in a baking dish, preferably shallow.
Refrigerate.
When ready To bake, Top with cheese
  and paprika. Place in 350° oven,
  uncovered, for 40 minutes or
  until hot Through and cheese is
  melted.
  Serves 8

Notes

Cambridge Chicken with Ham

Another "day ahead" one!

1 large fryer, cut in pieces
   flour, mixed with a little salt and pepper
¼ lb. butter or margarine
¼ cup chopped green onions
1 4-oz. can mushrooms, drained
1 slice ham, diced
1 clove garlic, minced
   pinch of Thyme
   salt and pepper To Taste
1 cup red wine

Shake chicken piece by piece in a paper bag
   containing The flour.
Brown chicken in butter and place in
   casserole.
Mix Together all The remaining ingredients
   and pour over chicken. Spoon The juice
   over the chicken so it is well saturated.
Bake, covered, in a 350° oven for 1 hour.

Remove and cool for a short Time before
   placing in the refrigerator over night.
The next day, when ready To bake, again
   spoon The liquid over The chicken and
   place, covered, in a 300° oven for 1 hour.

Serves 4

Notes

Family Dinner for Four

Meat, potatoes, and vegetables, all in one!

1 lb lean ground chuck
    salt and pepper to taste
4 medium sized potatoes
    sliced onions, according to your taste
½ Teasp. Worcestershire Sauce
1 large can solid pack Tomatoes

Brown the meat with the onions and add
    salt and pepper.
Peel potatoes and slice them into a 2 qt.
    casserole.
Place meat and onions on top of potatoes.
Add Worcestershire to the tomatoes —
    do not drain them — and pour
    this over all.
Refrigerate.

When ready to bake, place in 350° oven,
    covered, for 1½ hours or until potatoes
    are done.
Note: If you want to be fancier, you
    may add 2 cups diced celery and
    ½ cup diced green pepper. Arrange
    in layers with the potatoes.

Serves 4

Notes

Sophisticated Stew

A real "company" dish!

3 lbs lean round or chuck cut into large bite size pieces
  paper bag of flour seasoned with salt and pepper
6 strips of bacon
2 cloves of garlic, finely minced
1 oz. brandy, warmed
12 small whole fresh mushrooms
1 cup condensed beef bouillon
1½ cups dry red wine
12 small peeled white onions
12 small carrots, sliced
6 slightly bruised peppercorns
4 whole cloves
1 bay leaf, crumbled
2 Tblsp. chopped fresh parsley
¼ Teasp. dried marjoram
¼ Teasp. Thyme

Shake beef cubes in the flour, a few at a time until they are well covered.
In a large iron skillet fry the bacon until it begins to brown but is not crisp. Cut bacon into one inch pieces after cooking. Place in earthenware or heavy glass baking dish.

Cont'd 10

Notes

Sophisticated Stew (Cont'd)

Cook the garlic a little in the bacon-fat.

Then add the floured beef cubes and brown quickly on all sides, turning often.

Pour the brandy into the skillet, light it, and when flame dies out, remove the meat and garlic and put them in the casserole. (Garlic has probably disappeared by now.)

Put the mushrooms in skillet and brown lightly. Add them to casserole.

Put the bouillon and one cup of the red wine into skillet - bring to a boil and stir from the bottom to loosen the particles, using a wire whip. Pour the liquid into the casserole.

Add to the casserole the onions, carrots, peppercorns, cloves, bay leaf, parsley, marjoram, and thyme.

Now pour over the casserole your remaining ½ cup of red wine.

Cover the casserole tightly and bake at 300° for 2 hours. Cool, and place in refrigerator, covered.

When ready the next day, spoon some of the liquid up from the bottom over the meat and again place the casserole in a 300° oven, covered, and bake for 1 hour or until piping hot.

Serves 6

Notes

Chinese Casserole

The unusual flavor and crunchiness of this dish give it a personality all its own.

2 cans solid pack Tuna
1 can mushroom soup
1/4 cup water
1 Tblsp. soy sauce
1 cup whole cashew nuts
1 4-oz. can button mushrooms, drained
2 cups canned Chinese Chow Mein noodles
1/4 cup minced onion or chopped green onion Tops
1 cup chopped celery

Drain Tuna and break it into bite size chunks.
Mix Together the mushroom soup, water, and soy sauce.
Combine Tuna, mushroom soup mixture, and all remaining ingredients except 1 cup of the noodles.
Mix gently and place in casserole.
Refrigerate.

When ready To bake, sprinkle remaining cup of noodles on top and bake at 375°, uncovered, for 40 minutes.

Serves 6

Notes

Not Navy Beans

The best you ever ate!

1 pkg. dry red kidney beans - 1 lb. size
1 clove garlic, minced
1 ham end with plenty of meat on the
    bone - at least 3 lbs.
1 bottle chili sauce
½ bottle ketchup

Soak the beans overnight.
The next morning drain the beans, place
    them in a kettle, and cover them with
    water.
Add the garlic.
Add ham end, skin and all.
Simmer beans until they begin to soften -
    about 3 hours. Add water if necessary
    during cooking to keep beans covered. Don't
    worry if beans burst!
Remove ham end. Take off the skin. Remove
    meat from bone and cut in large bite size
    chunks. Return chunks to the beans.
    Simmer one hour more.
Drain beans except for about 1 cup bean liquor.
Add chili and ketchup to beans and mix gently.
Reheat slowly about 20 minutes until piping hot.
May be refrigerated and reheated - but keep it
    moist by adding more ketchup. Heat slowly!
Serves 6 to 8

13

Notes

Long Beach Seafood

A certain hit – and so easy!

2 cans frozen shrimp soup
2 Tblsp. sherry
2 small cans button mushrooms, drained
1 pkg. slivered almonds (about 2½ oz.)
½ lb. fresh crabmeat
½ lb. fresh shrimp, small size
   Sliced American cheese
   paprika

Melt soup according to directions on the
   can. Melt only – don't add milk or water!
Place melted soup in 2 qt. casserole and
   stir in sherry, mushrooms, and almonds.
Fold in seafood gently and cover with one
   layer of sliced cheese (not just one slice!)
Sprinkle paprika on top.

Refrigerate.

When ready to bake, place in 300° oven,
   uncovered, for one hour. Serve over
   hot fluffy rice.
Note: Lobster and prawns may be used as
   substitutes. Frozen seafood may be
   used if you cannot obtain fresh.
Serves 6

Notes

Easy Chicken Casserole

"Easy" is right!

1 cup uncooked rice
1 can mushroom soup
1 pkg. dehydrated onion soup
1 1/2 soup cans of milk
1 large fryer, cut in serving pieces
   salt and pepper

Mix together the rice, soups, and
   milk. Place in a large casserole.
   (I use a 3 qt. size)
Put the chicken on top, skin side
   down and add salt and pepper
   to taste.

Make this 3 hours ahead of time.
   Place it in a 250° oven, uncovered,
   for 3 hours. Turn the chicken
   over once. That's all!

Serves 4

Notes

Spaghetti Sauce

Everyone has her favorite, and this is mine.
  Yes—I know you'll say I used everything
  but the kitchen sink!

2 lbs lean ground beef
2 cloves garlic, minced
½ cup red wine
1 can mushrooms, undrained
1 pkg. dehydrated onion soup (1½ oz.)
2 teasp crushed basil leaves
½ teasp. salt
¼ teasp. pepper
  large pinch cinnamon
  large pinch allspice
3 tblsp. chopped fresh parsley
1 large can solid pack tomatoes, undrained
1 can tomato paste (6 oz. size)
1 cup water — more or less depending on
  the consistency you want.

Brown meat and garlic in large iron frying pan.
Add wine and simmer, stirring often, for 10
  minutes.
Add all remaining ingredients.
Cover pan almost completely (allowing space
  for steam to escape) and simmer 1 hour.
Toss with 12 oz. of steaming hot spaghetti
  and serve 8 hungry people.
This may be made ahead and refrigerated—or
  frozen—or just made when desired.

Notes

Mixed Bean Salad

Ideal for a barbecue. A wonderfully
  "fool-proof" recipe!

1 can green beans - No. 303 size (2 cups)
1 can wax beans - Same size
1 can red kidney beans - Same size
1/2 cup chopped green pepper
3/4 cup sugar
2/3 cup cider vinegar
1/3 cup salad oil
1 Teasp. pepper
1 Teasp. salt

Drain canned beans well.
Add chopped green pepper To beans.
Combine remaining ingredients and
  mix well.
Now mix all Together and let stand,
  refrigerated, for 24 hours.
Drain off excess liquid before serving.

Serves 6 generously.

Notes

Parsley Dressing for Fresh Tomatoes

Entirely different - and can be made days ahead.

2 cups fresh parsley
1/2 cup chopped chives
1 cup sweet pickles, drained
2 cloves garlic
salt and pepper to suit

Cut the chives very fine (I use scissors)

Then put all the above ingredients through the food grinder twice. Use the small blade. Save any juice that may escape.

Then add:
　　1/2 cup olive oil
　　1/2 cup red wine vinegar
　　1/4 cup Tarragon vinegar
　　　The juice from grinding

Mix all well and keep at room temperature for 24 hours in a covered jar. Then refrigerate.

Serve ice cold on platter of chilled, peeled, sliced tomatoes.

Will keep, refrigerated, covered for 2 weeks.

Notes

Lewiston Salad Dressing

My mother's favorite! Good on any kind of salad.

Juice of one large lemon, strained
6 Tblsp. olive oil (no substitute)
1 Teasp. salt
½ Teasp. pepper
½ clove garlic - if desired.

Mix in the order given and stir well.
Make it several hours ahead of time
    and let stand at room temperature.
When ready to serve, remove the
    garlic and again stir the
    dressing well.

For a salad serving 4 persons.

19

Notes

Coronado Salad Ring

So delicious and complete that it needs
no dressing.

1 pkg. lime jello
1 pkg. lemon jello
2 cups hot water
10 oz. dry creamed cottage cheese (small curd)
1 #2 can crushed pineapple, well drained
2/3 cup chopped walnuts
1 cup pastry cream, not whipped
1 cup mayonnaise
1 Tblsp. horseradish (bottled type)

Dissolve the jellos in the hot water.
Add remaining ingredients in the
    order given.
Place in a wet ring mold and
    refrigerate until firm.
When ready to serve, unmold onto
    a platter. Fill center with fresh
    strawberries.

Serves 8

Notes

Spinach Salad

Different! And so healthy!

2 cellophane pkgs. fresh spinach
  salad oil
  lemon juice

Wash spinach - shake gently to dry - cut off all stems.

Then, using scissors, cut spinach leaves in one inch wide pieces.

Sprinkle a little oil on leaves - Then a little lemon juice. Barely dampen the leaves - do not saturate!

Refrigerate.

Serve with a side dish of:

Chili Dressing

  1 cup mayonnaise
  1/4 cup chili sauce
  juice of 1 lemon
  minced green onion to taste

Mix well and chill until ready to serve.

Serves 6 to 8

Notes

Butterscotch Toffee Heavenly Delight

As good as it sounds!

1 1/2 cups whipping cream
1 can (5 1/2 oz.) butterscotch syrup (Topping)
1/2 Teasp. vanilla extract
1 unfrosted angel cake (9 1/2")
3/4 lb. English Toffee, crushed (put Through
    food grinder using largest blade.)

Whip cream until it starts To Thicken.
Add butterscotch syrup and vanilla slowly
    and continue beating until Thick.
Cut cake into 3 layers- horizontally.
Spread The butterscotch mixture on The
    layers and sprinkle each generously
    with crushed Toffee.
Put cake back Together again and frost
    The Top and sides with butterscotch
    mixture and sprinkle Them, Too,
    with Toffee.
Place cake in The refrigerator and
    chill for a minimum of 6
    hours.

Serves 12

Notes

Whiskey Ice Box Cake

A delectable dessert for 12.

2 envelopes gelatine
1/2 cup cold water
1/2 cup boiling water
6 eggs, separated
7 or 8 Tblsp. whiskey
1 cup sugar
1 Teasp. lemon juice
1 pt. whipping cream
3 pkgs. lady fingers, split

Soak gelatine in cold water. Then add
    boiling water and dissolve.
Beat egg yolks until thick.
Add whiskey very slowly.
Beat in the sugar.
Add lemon juice
Stir in gelatine and chill a short time.
Whip cream and fold it in.
Beat egg whites and fold in.
    Line sides and bottom of a springform
    pan (about 12") with split lady fingers.
Pour the mixture in slowly. When about
    half way, put in layer of lady fingers.
Then, when filled, place a layer of lady fingers
    on top in a design.
Chill overnight in the refrigerator.

23

Notes

Annapolis Angel Food Dessert

Hard on your dieting guests, but
   They'll never resist it!

2 bags chocolate bits
6 Teasp. warm water
3 eggs, separated
3 Tblsp. powdered sugar
½ cup chopped walnuts
1 ½ cups whipping cream
1 unfrosted angel cake (9½")

Melt chocolate bits in top of double boiler.
Add water and stir to mix. When all is
   melted and mixed, remove from fire.
Beat egg yolks with powdered sugar and
   add to chocolate mixture slowly.
Add chopped nuts. (Don't give up! This
   is usually hard to mix!)
Beat egg whites until stiff and fold into
   above mixture.
Whip cream and fold it in.
Place frosting in refrigerator for 12 hours.
Cut angel cake horizontally into 3 layers.
   Cover each layer with frosting - reassemble
   cake - frost top and sides and place in
   refrigerator for another 12 hours.

Serves 12   24

Notes

Bremerton Bourbon Balls

No-cook cookies!

2½ cups crushed vanilla wafers
   (Most of a 12. oz. pkg.)
2 Tblsp. cocoa
1 cup confectioners sugar (sift before measuring.)
1 cup chopped walnuts
3 Tblsp corn syrup or honey
¼ cup bourbon or brandy or rum
   confectioners sugar for Topping

Mix well The crumbs, cocoa, The
   1 cup sugar, and The nuts.
Add The corn syrup and liquor. Mix
   all very Thoroughly.
Form into one inch balls, Then roll
   in confectioners sugar. That's
   all!

Note: Keep in a covered Tin. These
   are even better The second day.

Makes 3 To 3½ dozen cookies.

25

Notes

Creme Chocolate

Fun To serve in after dinner coffee cups!

1 pkg. chocolate bits
4 Tblsp. cold water
5 eggs, separated
  whipped cream

Put chocolate bits in pan with The
  cold water. Stir over low heat, with
  wooden spoon, until well blended.
Remove from The fire and slowly stir
  in The 5 egg yolks which have
  been well beaten. Mix well.
Fold in The 5 stiffly beaten whites.
  Continue until all is well blended.
Pour into after dinner coffee cups and
  store in refrigerator at least 5
  hours- preferably overnight.
Serve in cups with a bit of whipped
  cream - unsweetened, as This is a
  very rich dessert.
Fills 10 cups.

Notes

Pasadena Peach Delight

The perfect dessert for a hot summer evening! And particularly good after seafood.

1 pkg. ladyfingers (about 10)
Peach Brandy
2 pkgs. frozen sliced peaches (semi-thawed)
½ pint whipping cream
1 teasp. sugar
4 or 5 drops vanilla or almond extract

Line bottom and sides of ice cube tray with split ladyfingers.
Moisten ladyfingers with brandy but do not saturate.
Arrange partly thawed peach slices over ladyfingers.
Whip cream, adding sugar and flavoring.
Top the dessert with whipped cream.
If you wish to be extra fancy, sprinkle top of whipped cream with toasted slivered almonds.
Cover ice tray with wax paper and freeze for at least 6 hours.
When serving, cut across tray to form narrow slices. (Remove from freezer.
Serves 8   20 minutes before serving.)

Notes

Washington Cookies

Our favorites!

1½ cups flour
1 Teasp. soda
1 Teasp. salt
1 cup margarine
3/4 cup brown sugar
3/4 cup granulated sugar

2 eggs
1 Teasp. vanilla
1 cup chopped walnuts
2 cups rolled oats
1 pkg. chocolate bits

Sift flour, measure, and sift again with soda and salt.

Cream margarine with both sugars.

Beat eggs into margarine-sugar mixture. Add vanilla and mix well.

Stir in dry ingredients.

Add nuts, oats, and bits and mix all thoroughly.

Drop on greased cookie sheet (about 1 Tblsp. batter for each cookie) and bake 12-15 minutes at 350° until light brown.

Makes about 6 dozen delicious cookies.

Notes

Quick but Tasty Desserts with no Advance Preparation

It's easy to keep the ingredients for several of these on hand ready for unexpected guests.

1. Top a chilled slice of pineapple with a scoop of pineapple ice. Make a slight indentation on top of ice and pour in 2 or 3 Tblsp. Creme de Menthe.

2. Top coffee ice cream with grated semi-sweet chocolate.

3. Top a serving of vanilla ice cream with several Tblsp. of Cointreau.

4. Top mocha ice cream with hot chocolate sauce.

5. Top lime ice with crushed chocolate bits.

6. Top a saucer of fresh raspberries with several Tblsp. commercial sour cream. Top sour cream with one half Tblsp. brown sugar.

Notes

Filled French Rolls

Fun to make - and fun to eat!

8 French rolls
1/2 cup softened margarine - not melted
1/2 cup grated Parmesan cheese
2 Tblsp. salad oil
1/2 cup finely chopped fresh parsley
1 clove garlic, finely chopped
1/2 Teasp. sweet basil
    salt to taste

Turn each roll on its side and cut into
    1/2 inch slices - but do not cut all the
    way through the roll.
Make the filling by blending the margarine
    with the remaining ingredients.
Spread the filling between each slice.
Wrap each roll individually in aluminum
    foil. Set aside until needed.

Bake in a 375° oven for 20 minutes.
Serve in the foil. Each person keeps his
    roll hot by rewrapping in the foil.
    Wonderful for a barbecue in your
    patio!
Rolls may be frozen in their foil wrappers.
    If not thawed, bake 10 minutes longer.

Notes

Cheese Roll

You'll love it!

1 lb. yellow cheese
2 pkg. cream cheese (3 oz. each)
1 cup cashew nuts
2 cloves garlic, minced
  paprika

Put yellow cheese through food grinder,
  using the finest blade.
Soften and whip the cream cheese.
Put cashews through grinder - same blade.
Mix all ingredients, except paprika, well.
Shape into a roll about 1 1/2 inches in
  diameter.
Then roll in lots of paprika. The roll
  should be really red on the outside.
Wrap in wax paper and refrigerate.
When ready to serve, slice very thin
  and place on round crackers.
This keeps well in your refrigerator
  or may be frozen.

31

Notes

Clam Canapes

One of my most used recipes.

1 pkg. cream cheese
1 can minced clams, drained
   salt to taste
   dash of red pepper
3/4 Teasp. Worcestershire Sauce
1 Teasp. minced green onion

Whip The cheese with a fork.
Add The clams and mix well.
Add remaining ingredients and
   whip well.
Place in the refrigerator in a
   covered dish.

When ready To serve, heap generously
   on plain white salty crackers and
   bake at 300° for 20 minutes.
You may sprinkle with paprika
   for "looks."

32

Notes

Double Cheese Dip

1 Triangle Roquefort cheese – or about
   1/3 cup Bleu cheese
2 pkgs. cream cheese (3 oz. size)
1 Tblsp. chopped fresh parsley
2 Tblsp. chopped green onions
   dash of cayenne
   dash of Worcestershire Sauce
2 heaping Tblsp. mayonnaise
4 level Tblsp. commercial sour cream
1/4 Teasp. horseradish
   salt To Taste

Cream cheeses Together.
Add remaining ingredients – mix well –
   do not refrigerate, just set aside.
When ready, serve with potato chips.

If you place This in The refrigerator
   for several hours, it will harden and
   become an excellent dip for carrot
   Sticks.

Notes

San Francisco Cocktail

Before a festive luncheon it is often fun to serve an unusual cocktail. Try this!

2 fifths of White Port
8 oz. light Rum
   juice of 4 lemons
   Maraschino cherries - or fresh strawberries

Chill the Port
Add the Rum and lemon juice
Mix well, place in a glass container
   and refrigerate.

When ready to serve, place a cherry
   or fresh strawberry in each glass,
   stir the cocktail well, and serve
   very cold in wine or martini
   glasses. You may add a little
   ice to the shaker to keep it
   cold.

Serves 12 - 16

Notes

Note

One half the author's profit from all 4 "Make It Now" books is given to:

The National Cystic Fibrosis Research Foundation
521 Fifth Avenue
New York, New York 10017

If you would like a copy of any of the other "Make It Now" books — which contain the same type recipes but come in different colors with matching envelopes — ask your local book or gift shop — or write for information to:

Cooper-Trent, Division of Keuffel & Esser Co.
1521 N. Danville St.
Arlington, Virginia 22201

Notes

Notes

Notes

Notes

Notes

Notes

Notes

Notes

Notes